SONGS FROM AND INSPIRED BY THE HIT TV SERIES

2   **The Best of Both Worlds**

6   **Who Said**

11   **Just Like You**

14   **Pumpin' Up the Party**

18   **If We Were a Movie**

24   **I Got Nerve**

28   **The Other Side of Me**

21   **This Is the Life**

32   **Pop Princess**

36   **She's No You**

48   **Find Yourself in You**

43   **Shining Star**

52   **I Learned from You**

ISBN 978-1-4234-3936-3

WALT DISNEY MUSIC COMPANY

DISTRIBUTED BY

HAL•LEONARD®
CORPORATION

7777 W. BLUEMOUND RD. P.O. BOX 13819 MILWAUKEE, WI 53213

In Australia Contact:
Hal Leonard Australia Pty. Ltd.
4 Lentara Court
Cheltenham, Victoria, 3192 Australia
Email: ausadmin@halleonard.com.au

Visit Hal Leonard Online at
www.halleonard.com

The Best of Both Worlds

Words and Music by Matthew Gerrard and Robbie Nevil

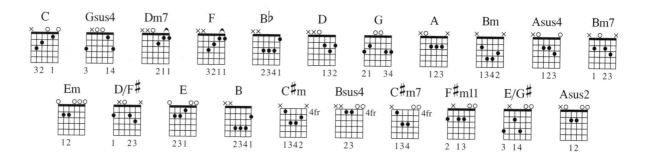

*Capo I

Strum Pattern: 3, 4

Pick Pattern: 3, 4

Intro

Moderately fast

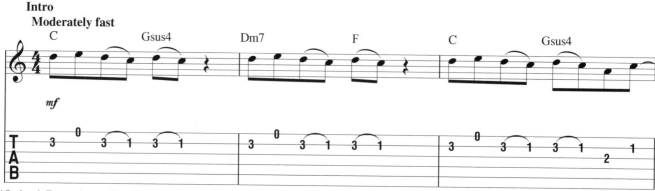

*Optional: To match recording, place capo at 1st fret.

Verse

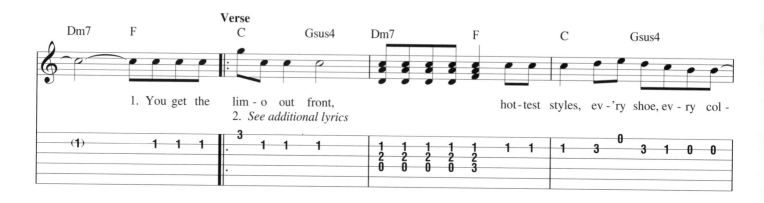

1. You get the lim-o out front,
2. *See additional lyrics*

hot-test styles, ev-'ry shoe, ev-ry col-

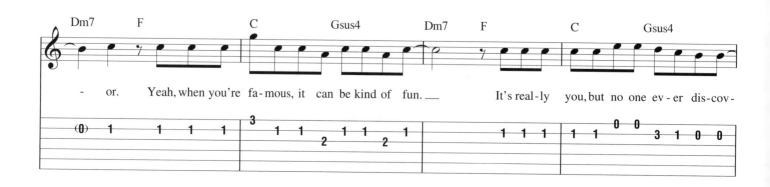

- or. Yeah, when you're fa-mous, it can be kind of fun. ___ It's real-ly you, but no one ev-er dis-cov-

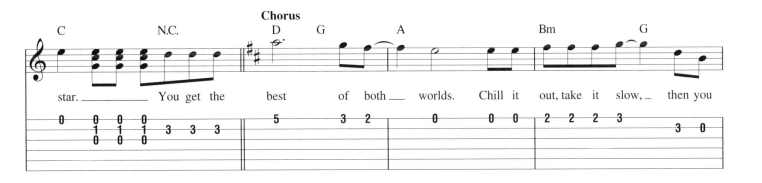

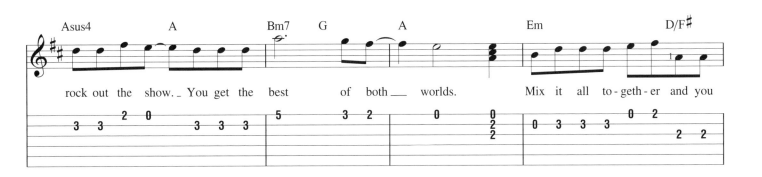

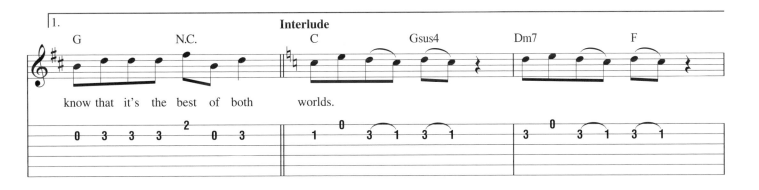

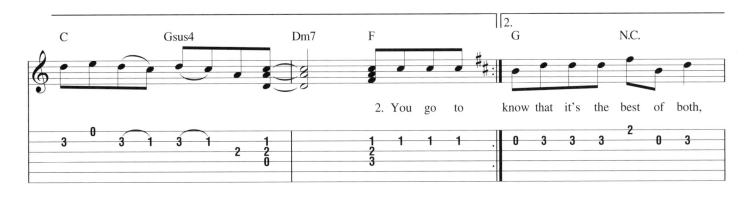

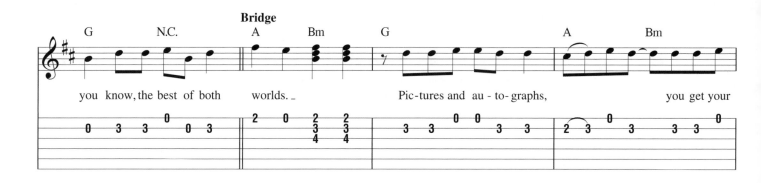

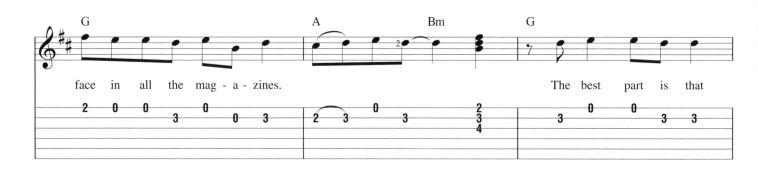

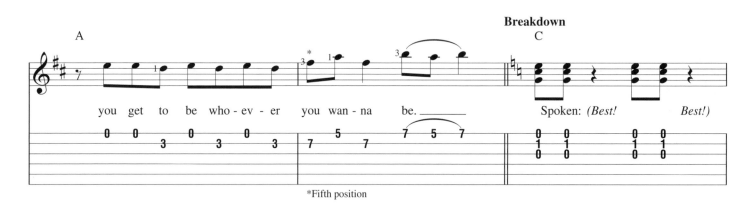

*Fifth position

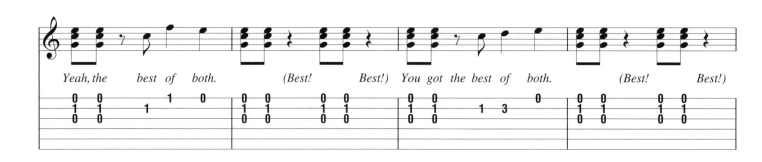

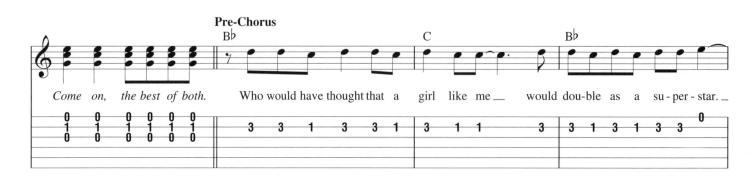

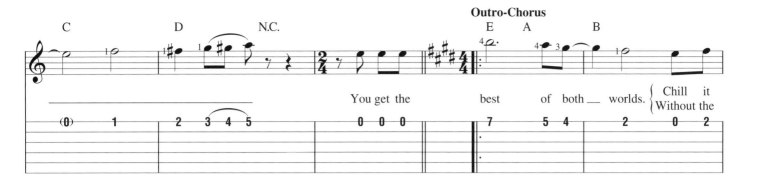

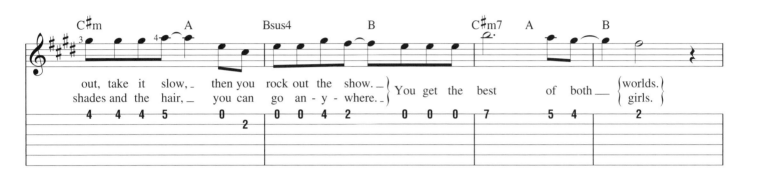

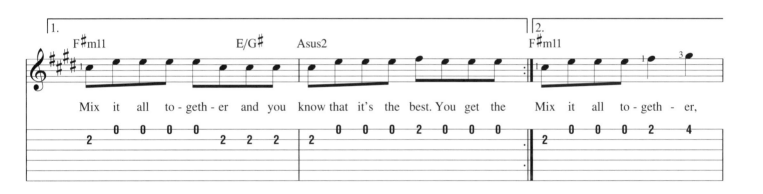

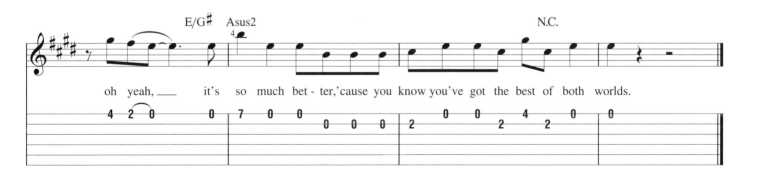

Additional Lyrics

2. You go to movie premiers,
   Hear your songs on the radio.
   Living two lives is a little weird,
   But school's cool, 'cause nobody knows.

Pre-Chorus Yeah, you get to be a small town girl,
   But big time when you play your guitar.

Who Said

Words and Music by Matthew Gerrard, Robbie Nevil and Jay Landers

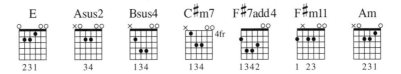

Strum Pattern: 1, 6
Pick Pattern: 2, 4

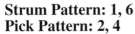

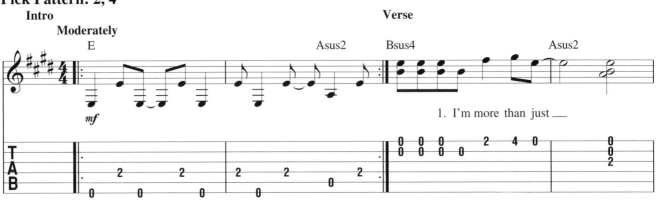

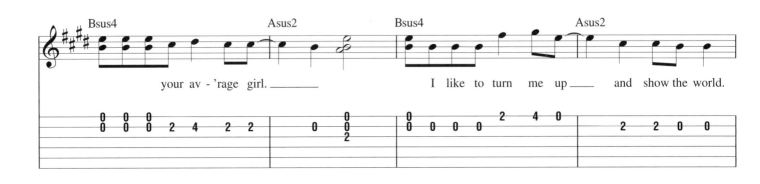

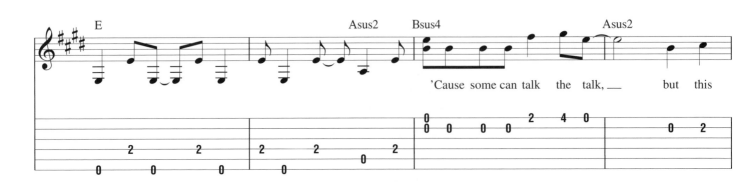

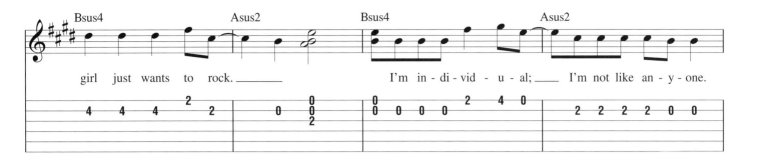

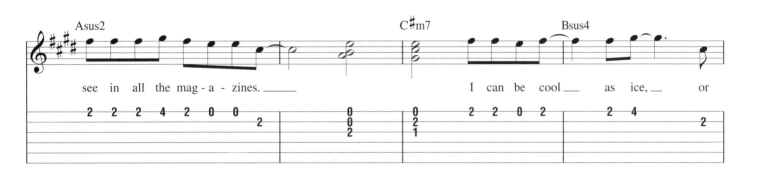

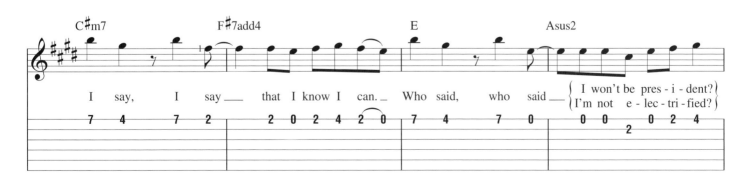

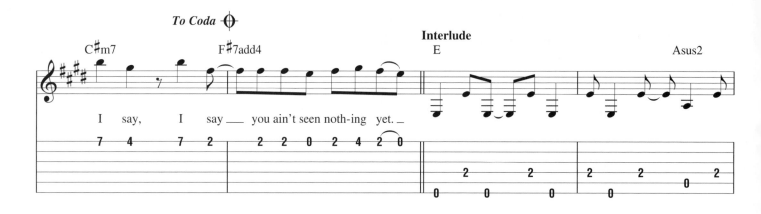

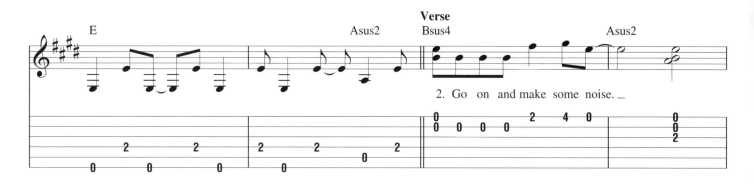

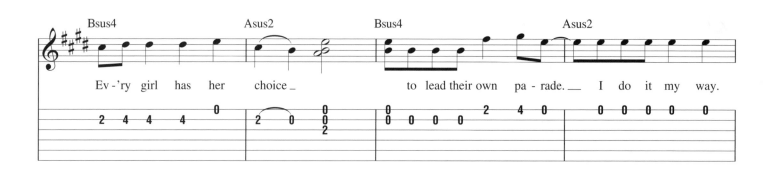

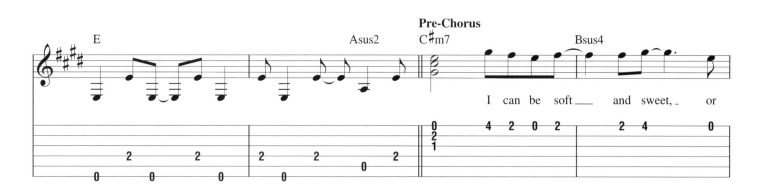

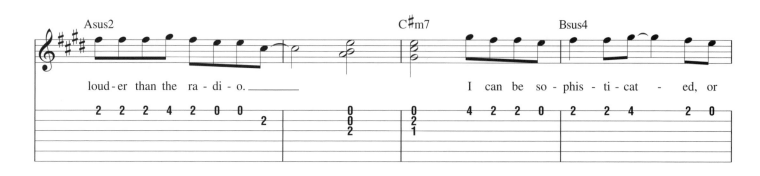

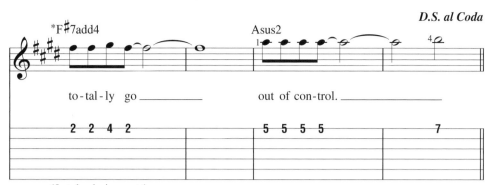

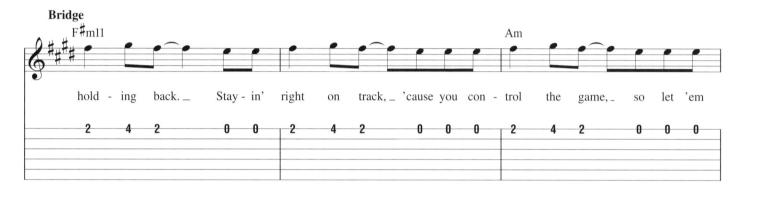

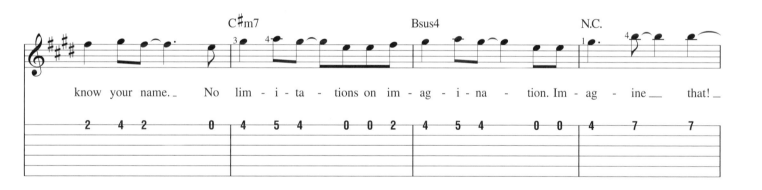

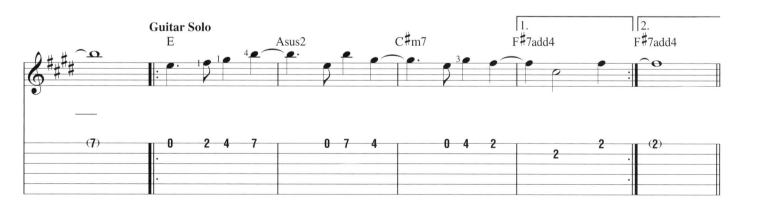

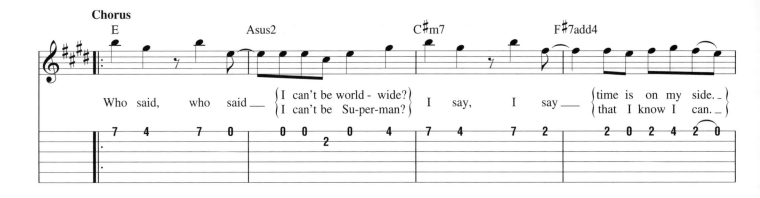

Chorus

Who said, who said ___ { I can't be world - wide? / I can't be Su-per-man? } I say, I say ___ { time is on my side. / that I know I can. }

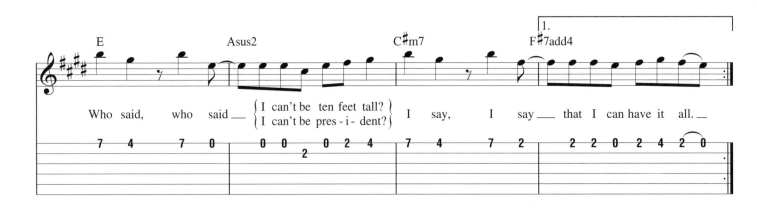

Who said, who said ___ { I can't be ten feet tall? / I can't be pres - i - dent? } I say, I say ___ that I can have it all. ___

1.

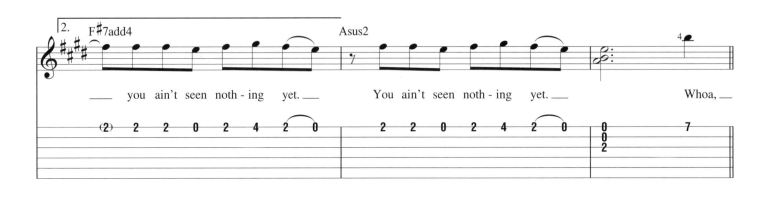

2. F#7add4   Asus2

___ you ain't seen noth - ing yet. ___ You ain't seen noth - ing yet. ___ Whoa,

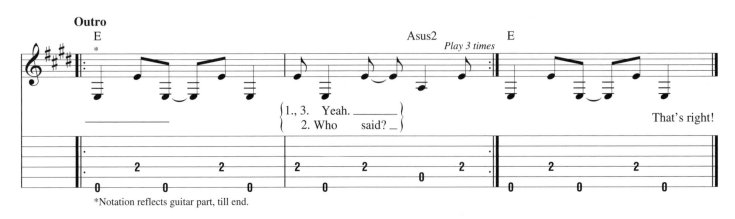

Outro

Play 3 times

{ 1., 3. Yeah. ___ / 2. Who said? ___ }

That's right!

*Notation reflects guitar part, till end.

10

Just Like You

Words and Music by Andrew Dodd and Adam Watts

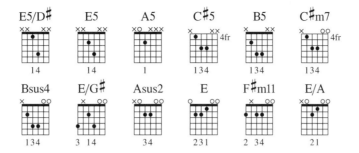

Strum Pattern: 1, 3
Pick Pattern: 1, 2

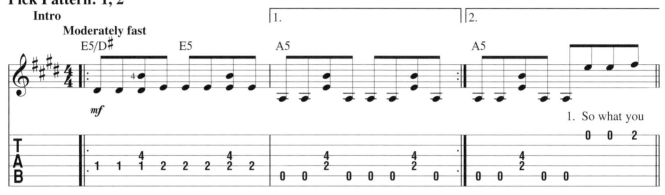

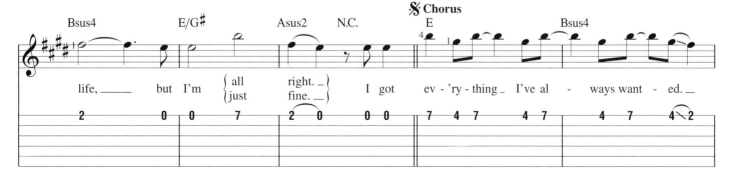

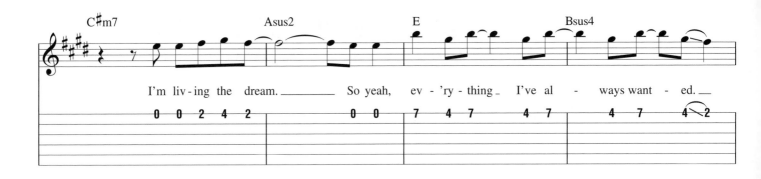

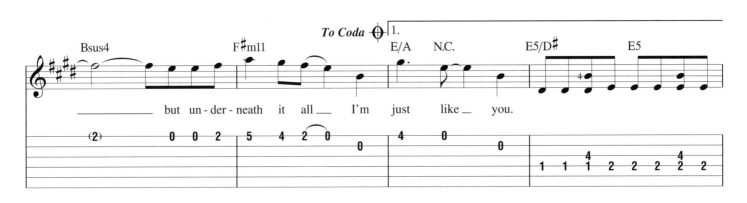

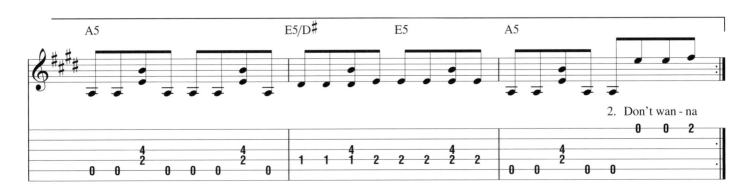

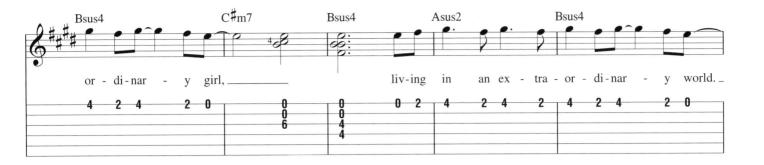

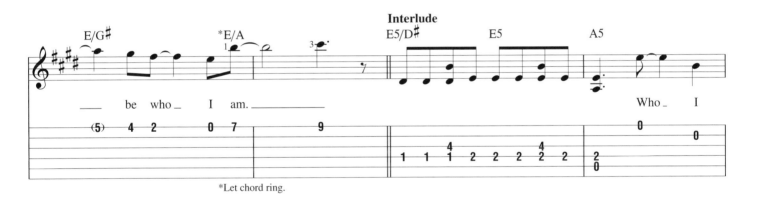

*Let chord ring.

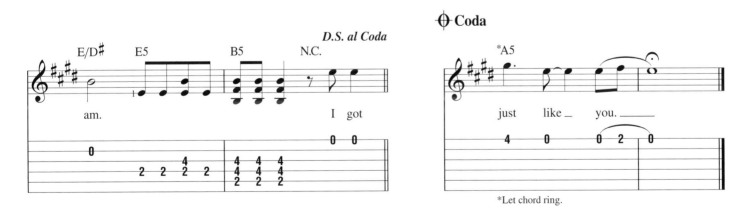

*Let chord ring.

Additional Lyrics

2. Don't wanna be treated diff'rently.
   I wanna keep it all inside.
   Half the time I've got my name in lights;
   The other half I'm by your side.

Pumpin' Up the Party

Words and Music by Jamie Houston

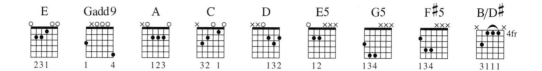

Strum Pattern: 3, 4
Pick Pattern: 1, 3

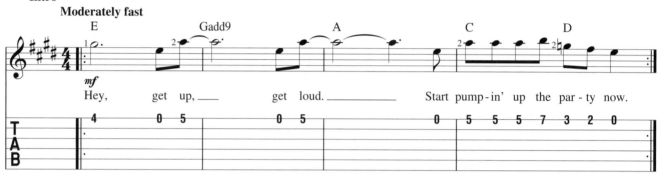

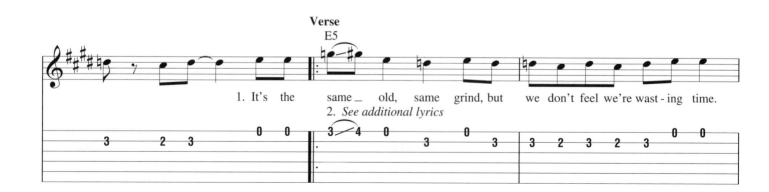

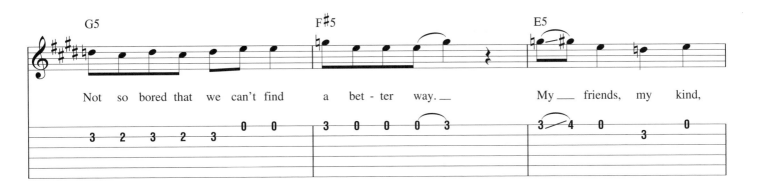

Not so bored that we can't find a bet-ter way. ___ My ___ friends, my kind,

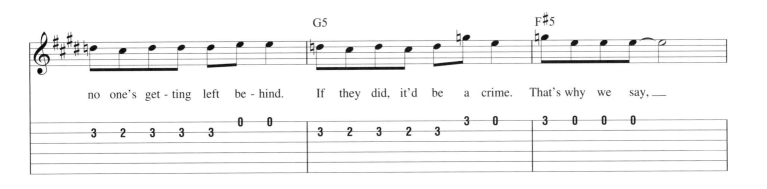

no one's get-ting left be - hind. If they did, it'd be a crime. That's why we say, ___

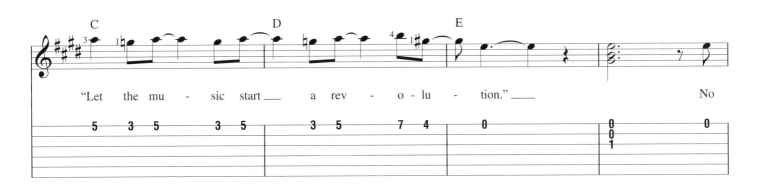

"Let the mu - sic start ___ a rev - o - lu - tion." ___ No

Chorus

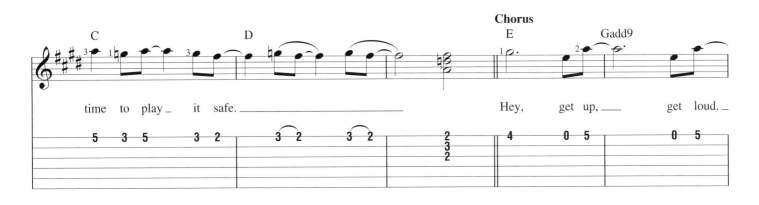

time to play ___ it safe. _____ Hey, get up, ___ get loud. ___

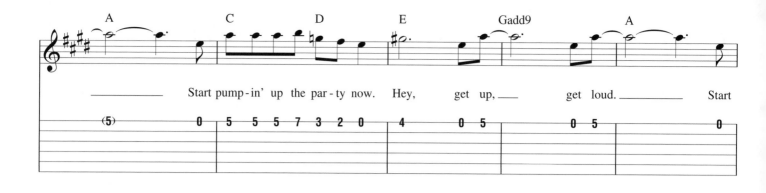

Start pump-in' up the par-ty now. Hey, get up, ___ get loud. ___ Start

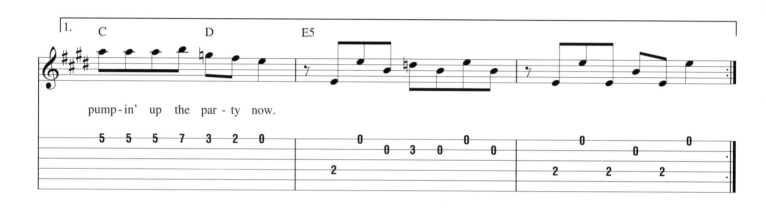

pump-in' up the par-ty now.

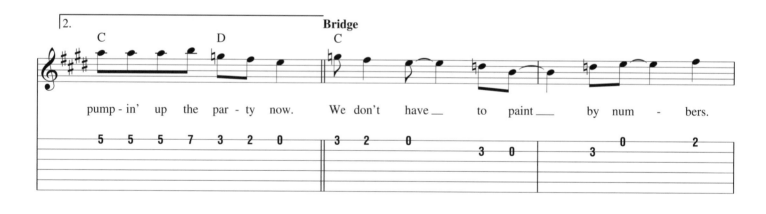

pump-in' up the par-ty now. We don't have ___ to paint ___ by num - bers.

Let our voice ___ come out ___ from un - der. Hear it rise, ___ feel ___ the thun - der. It's

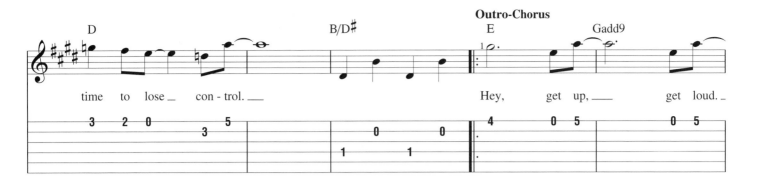

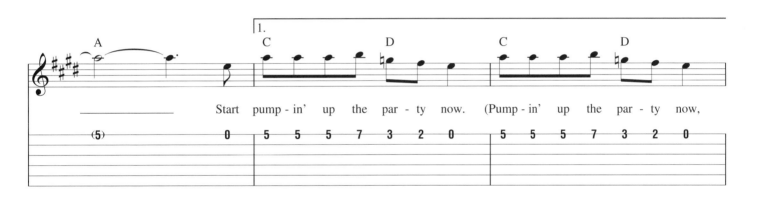

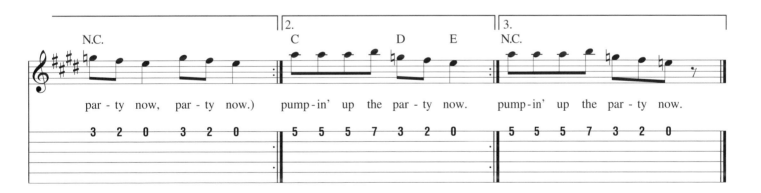

Additional Lyrics

2. They can't, we can.
   Parents might not understand
   Havin' fun without a plan,
   But that's what we do.
   We're all here. (Let's go!)
   Gotta make this party grow.
   Together we can make it grow
   Right through the roof.
   The music's gonna start a revolution.
   Too late to play it safe.

If We Were a Movie

Words and Music by Jeannie Lurie and Holly Mathis

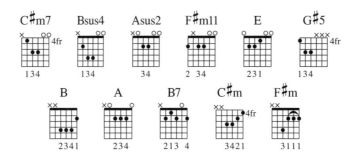

Strum Pattern: 2, 3
Pick Pattern: 3, 4

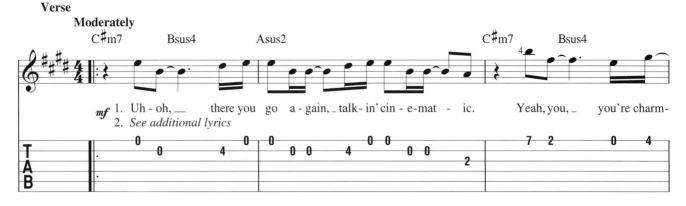

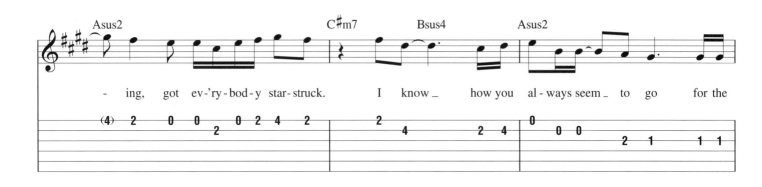

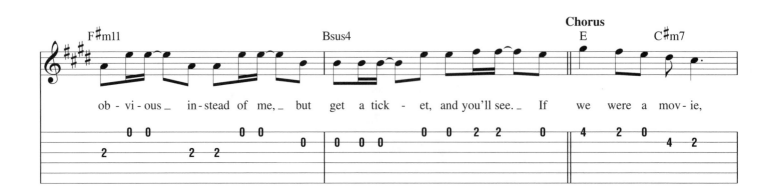

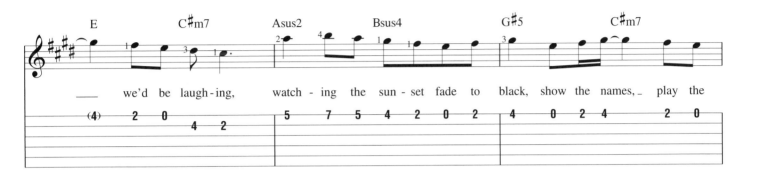

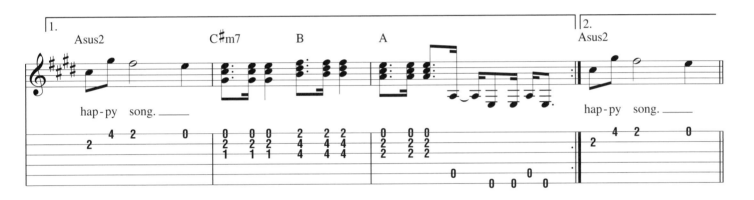

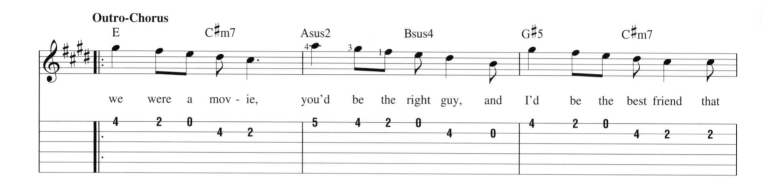

Additional Lyrics

2. Yeah, yeah, when you call me I can hear it in your voice.
Oh, sure, want to see me and tell me all about her.
La, la, I'll be acting through my tears.
Guess you'll never know that I should win an Oscar® for the scene I'm in.

This Is the Life

Words and Music by Jeannie Lurie and Shari Short

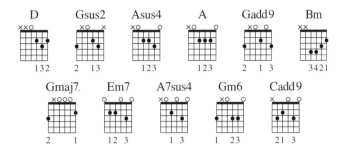

*Capo II

Strum Pattern: 6
Pick Pattern: 4, 6

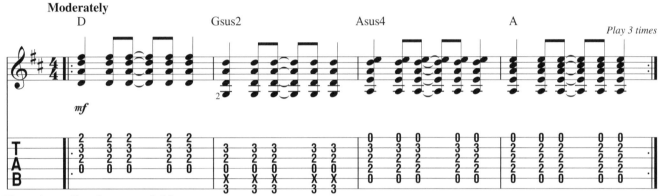

*To match recording, place capo at 2nd fret.

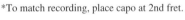

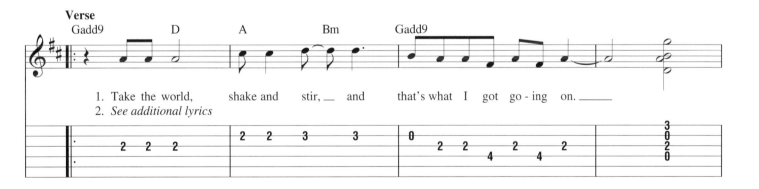

1. Take the world, shake and stir, __ and that's what I got go-ing on. ____
2. *See additional lyrics*

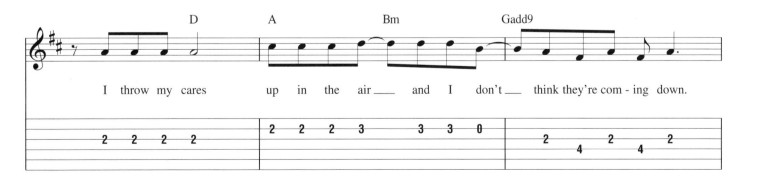

I throw my cares up in the air ___ and I don't ___ think they're com-ing down.

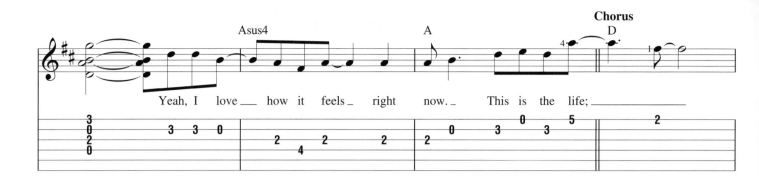

Yeah, I love ___ how it feels ___ right now. ___ This is the life; _____

hold on ___ tight. ___ And this is a dream. _____ It's all I ___ need. ___ You

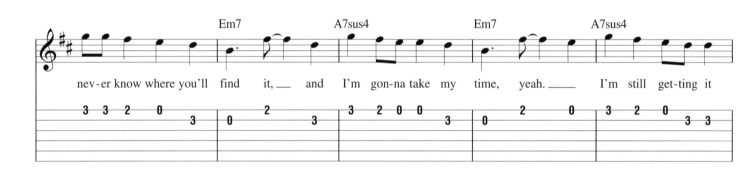

nev-er know where you'll find it, ___ and I'm gon-na take my time, yeah. _____ I'm still get-ting it

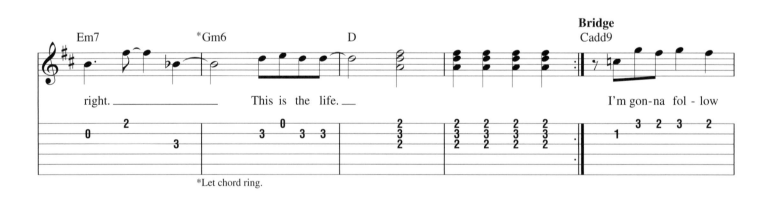

right. _____ This is the life. ___ I'm gon-na fol - low

*Let chord ring.

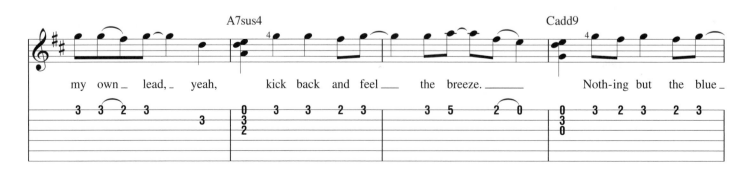

my own ___ lead, _ yeah, kick back and feel ___ the breeze. _____ Noth-ing but the blue ___

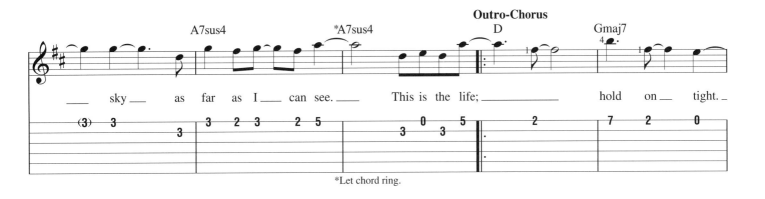

*Let chord ring.

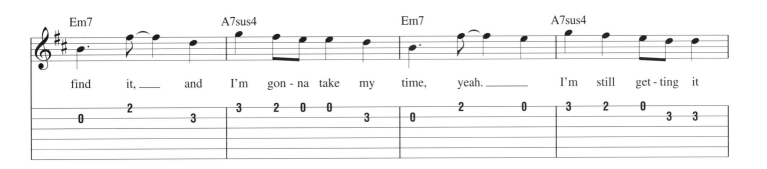

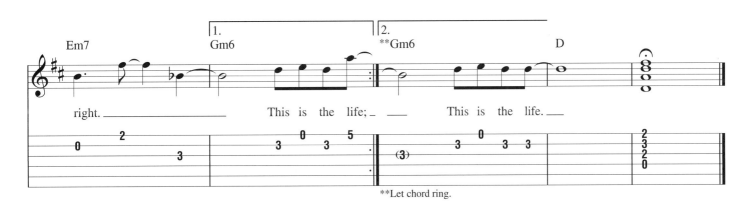

**Let chord ring.

Additional Lyrics

2. Takin' in a whole new scene,
And I'm swimming with a new crowd.
Breakin' down the old four walls
And I'm building them up from the ground.
Yeah, I love how it feels right now.

I Got Nerve

Words and Music by Jeannie Lurie, Ken Hauptman and Aruna Abrams

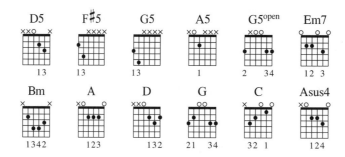

*Capo I

Strum Pattern: 1, 4
Pick Pattern: 4, 5

*Optional: To match recording, place capo at 1st fret.

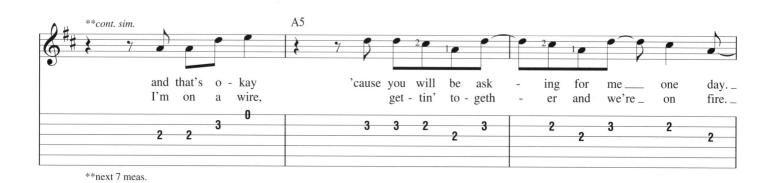

**next 7 meas.

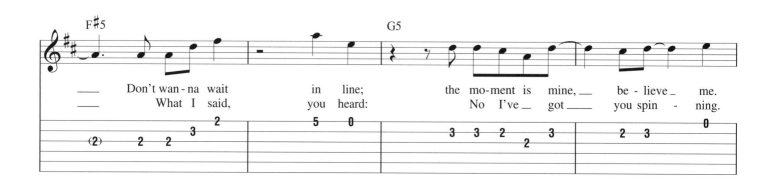

Pre-Chorus

Don't close ___ your eyes, ___ 'cause it's a chance ___ worth tak - ing,⎫
Don't close ___ your mind. ___ The words I use ___ are o - pen,⎭

and I think that I ___

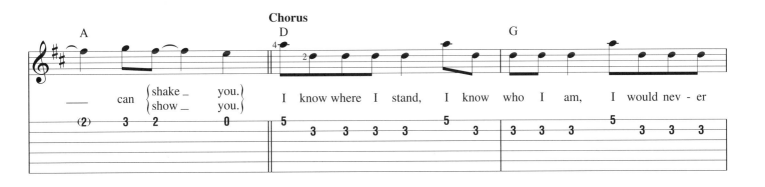

Chorus

___ can ⎰shake ___ you.⎱ I know where I stand, I know who I am, I would nev - er
        ⎱show ___ you.⎰

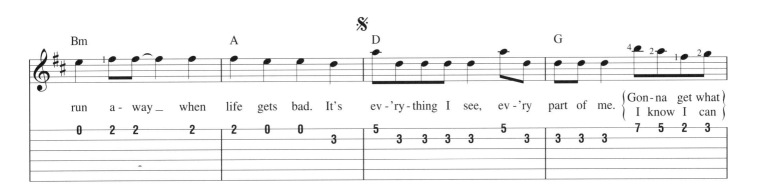

run a - way ___ when life gets bad. It's ev - 'ry-thing I see, ev - 'ry part of me. ⎰Gon - na get what⎱
                                                                                    ⎱I know I can⎰

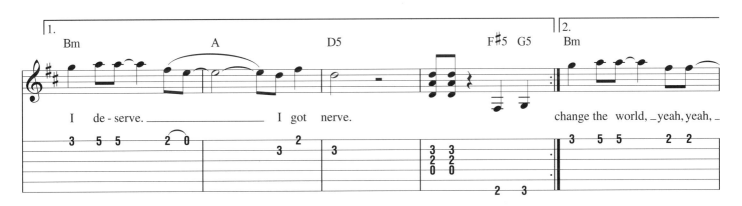

I de - serve. _____ I got nerve.   change the world, ___ yeah, yeah, ___

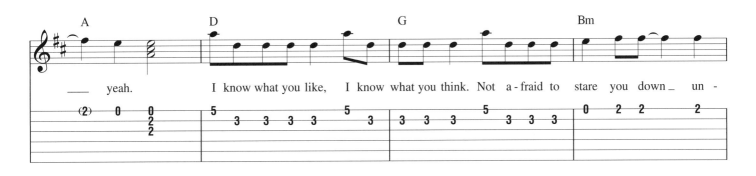

___ yeah.   I know what you like, I know what you think. Not a - fraid to stare you down ___ un -

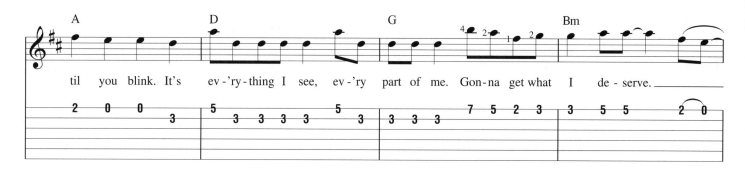

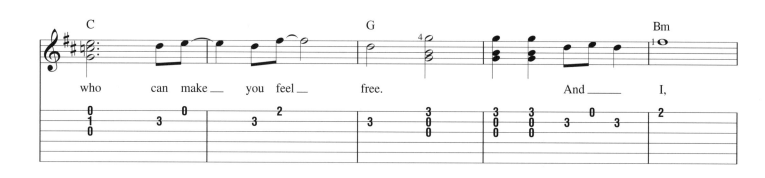

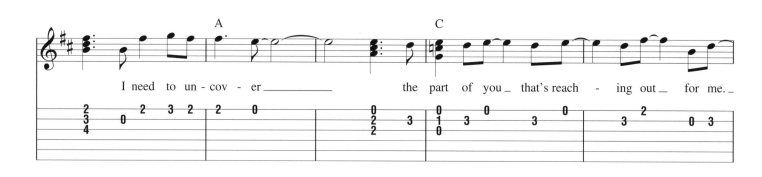

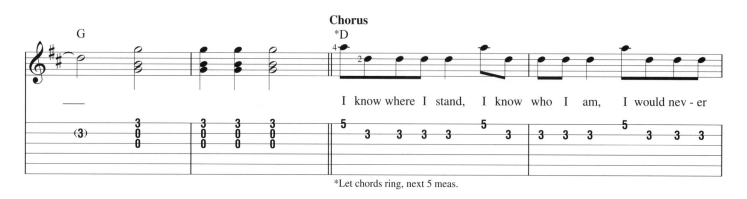

*Let chords ring, next 5 meas.

*Let chord ring.

The Other Side of Me

Words and Music by Matthew Gerrard, Robbie Nevil and Jay Landers

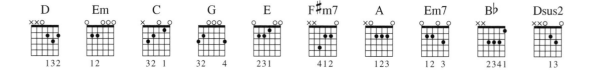

*Capo II

Strum Pattern: 3, 4
Pick Pattern: 1, 3

Intro
Moderately fast

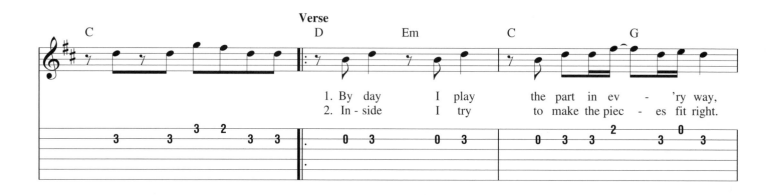

*Optional: To match recording, place capo at 2nd fret.

Verse

1. By day   I play   the part in ev - 'ry way,
2. In - side   I try   to make the piec - es fit right.

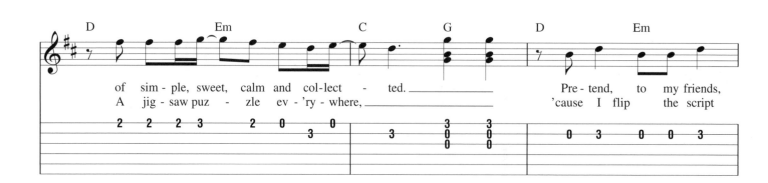

of sim - ple, sweet, calm and col - lect - ed. _____   Pre - tend, to my friends,
A jig - saw puz - zle ev - 'ry - where, _____   'cause I flip the script

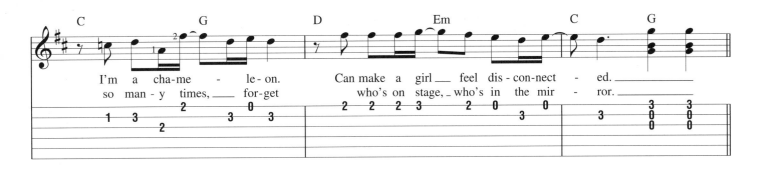

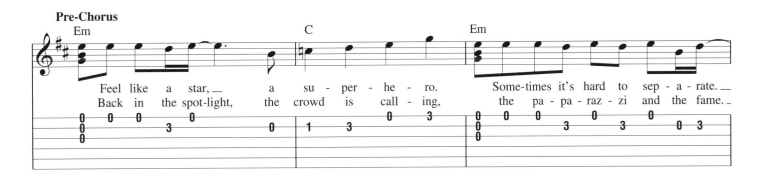

Pre-Chorus

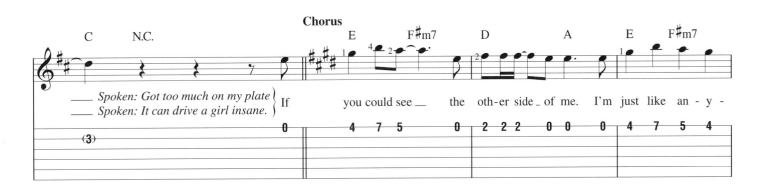

Chorus

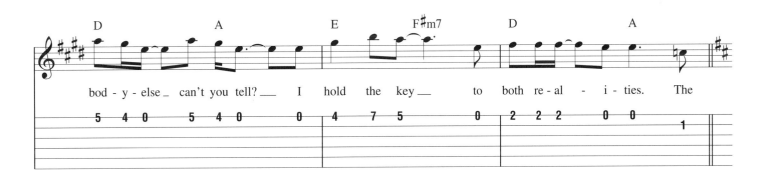

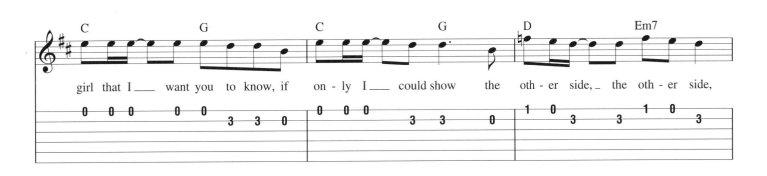

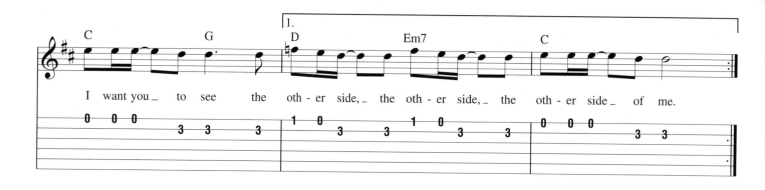

I want you _ to see the oth - er side, _ the oth - er side, _ the oth - er side _ of me.

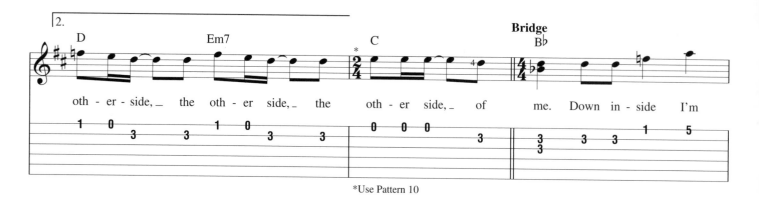

oth - er - side, _ the oth - er side, _ the oth - er side, _ of me. Down in - side I'm

*Use Pattern 10

not that dif - f'rent; like ev - 'ry - one, I have a dream. _ Don't wan - na hide, just

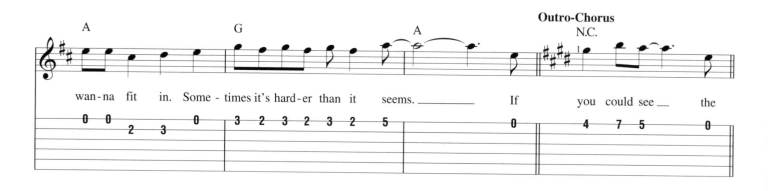

wan - na fit in. Some - times it's hard - er than it seems. _____ If you could see _ the

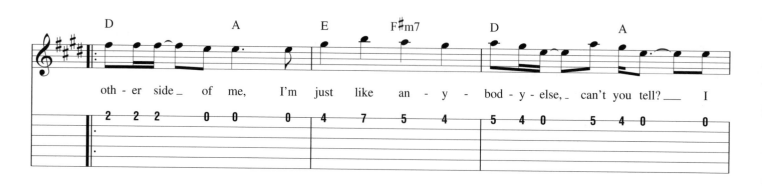

oth - er side _ of me, I'm just like an - y - bod - y - else, _ can't you tell? ___ I

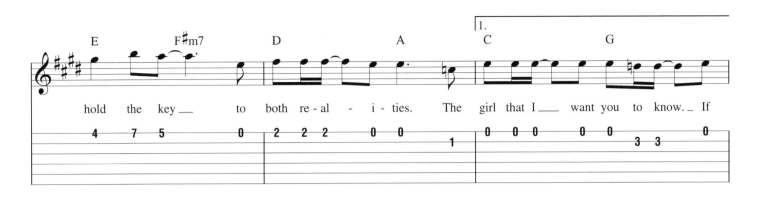

hold the key ___ to both re-al - i - ties. The girl that I ___ want you to know. ___ If

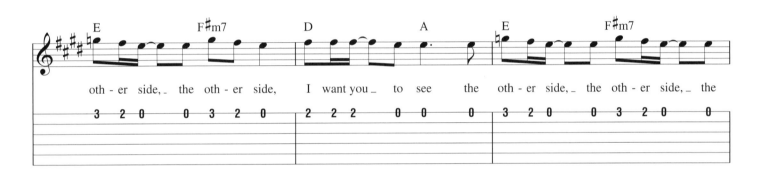

you could see ___ the girl that I ___ want you to know, ___ if on - ly I ___ could show the

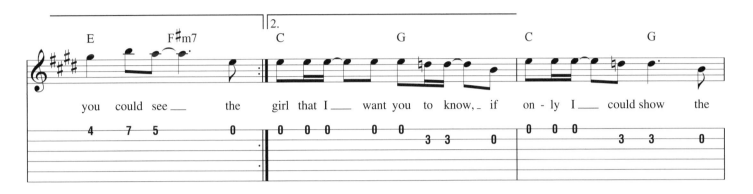

oth - er side, ___ the oth - er side, I want you ___ to see the oth - er side, ___ the oth - er side, ___ the

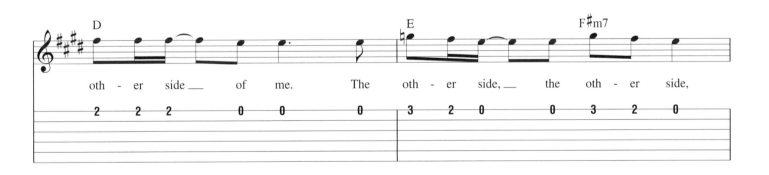

oth - er side ___ of me. The oth - er side, ___ the oth - er side,

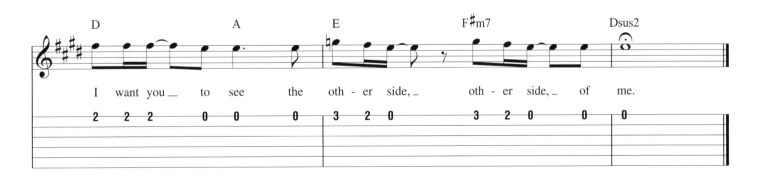

I want you ___ to see the oth - er side, ___ oth - er side, ___ of me.

Pop Princess

Words and Music by Ben Romans

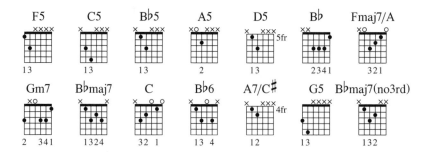

Strum Pattern: 1, 2
Pick Pattern: 2, 4

Intro
Moderately fast

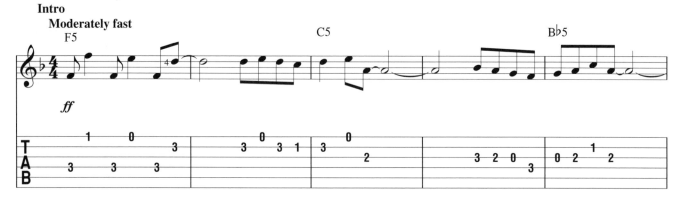

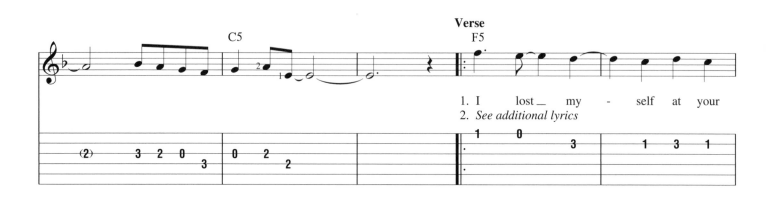

1. I lost my-self at your
2. *See additional lyrics*

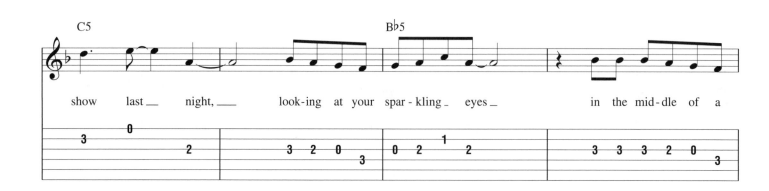

show last night, look-ing at your spar-kling eyes in the mid-dle of a

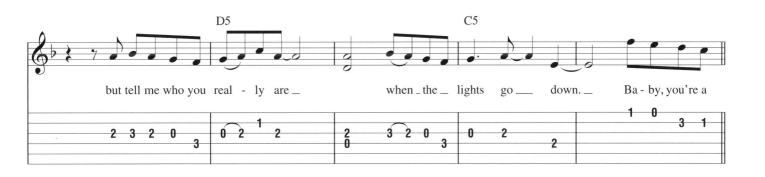

Pre-Chorus

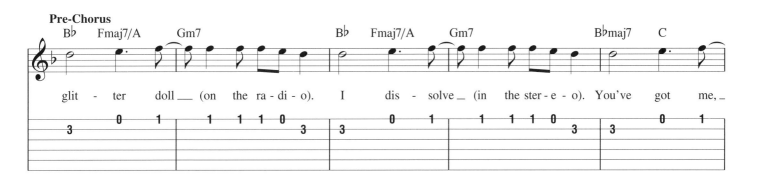

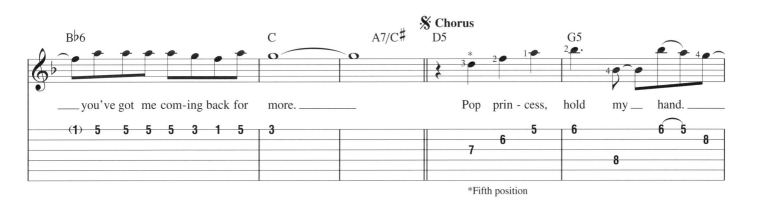

*Fifth position

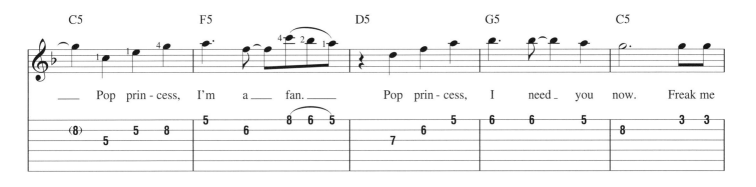

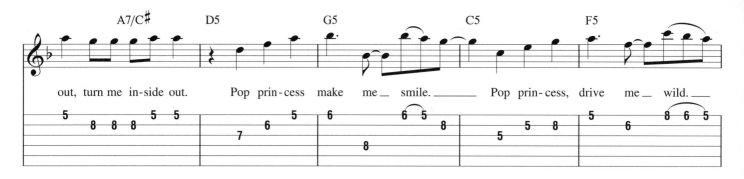

out, turn me in-side out.   Pop prin-cess make me_ smile.____ Pop prin-cess, drive me_ wild.__

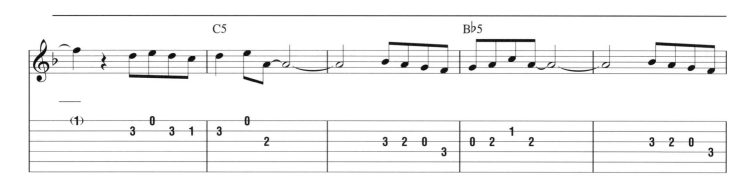

Pop prin-cess I need_ you now,   so ba - by, turn your love up   loud._____

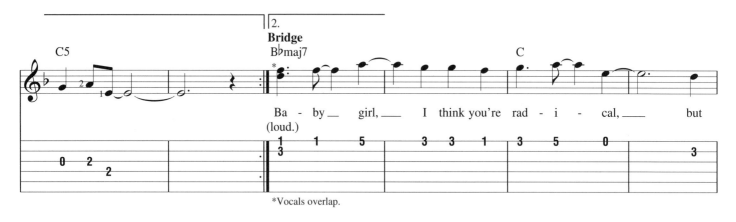

Ba - by_ girl,____ I think you're rad - i - cal,____ but
(loud.)

*Vocals overlap.

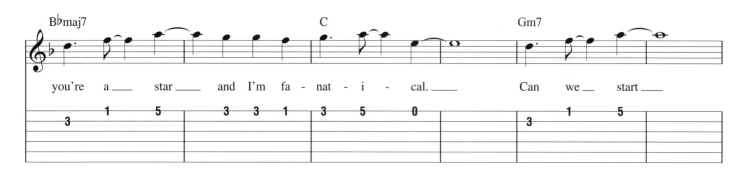

you're a _ star ____ and I'm fa - nat - i - cal. ____   Can we _ start ____

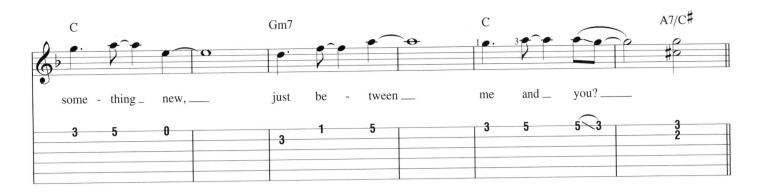

some - thing _ new, ___ just be - tween ___ me and _ you? ___

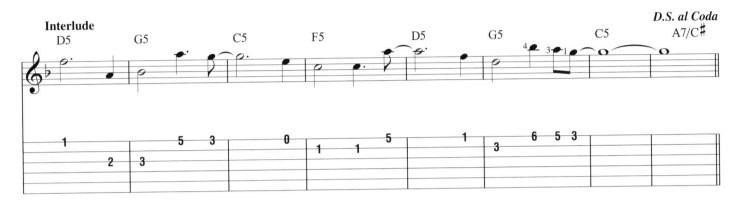

Interlude

D.S. al Coda

Coda

Outro

1., 2., 3.

loud. (Pop prin - cess, ___ pop prin - cess.) Ba - by, turn your love up

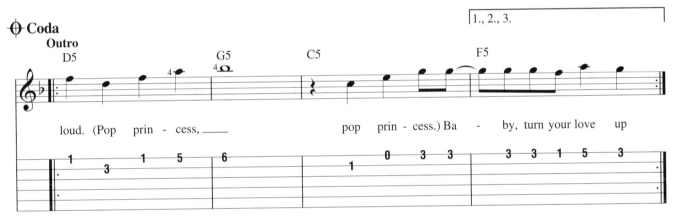

4.

- by, turn your love up loud. ___ *rit.*

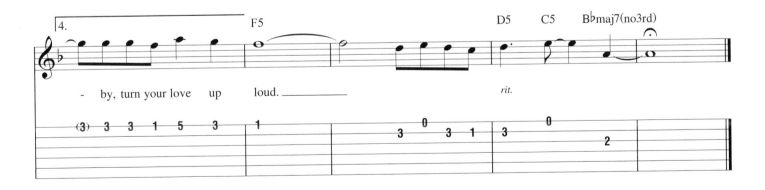

Additional Lyrics

2. You were hiding in a darkened stall,
   Waiting on your curtain call,
   Getting your piece of mind.
   But I was looking past the glossy stare.
   I knew who was really there,
   And I'd like to spend some time.

She's No You

Words and Music by Matthew Gerrard, Jesse McCartney and Robbie Nevil

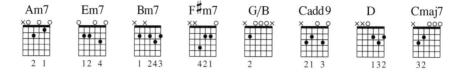

Strum Pattern: 3, 4
Pick Pattern: 2, 4

Intro
Moderately

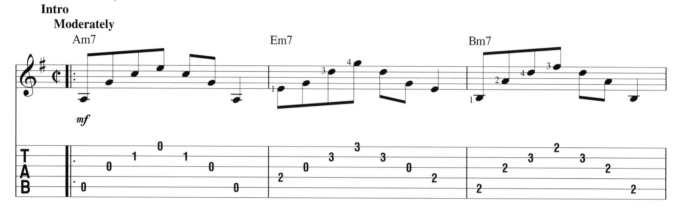

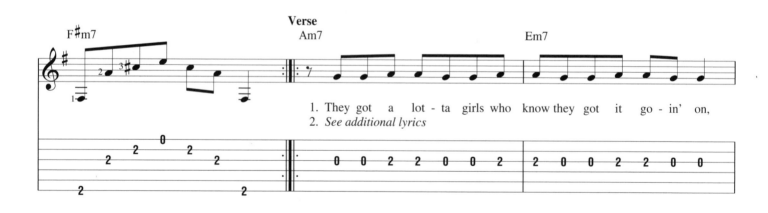

1. They got a lot-ta girls who know they got it go-in' on,
2. *See additional lyrics*

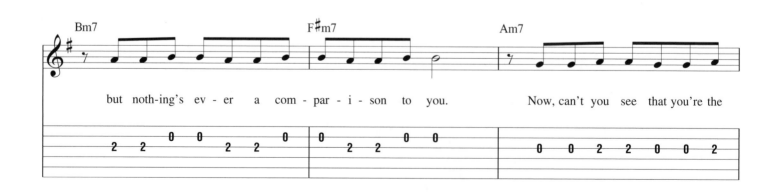

but noth-ing's ev-er a com-par-i-son to you.   Now, can't you see that you're the

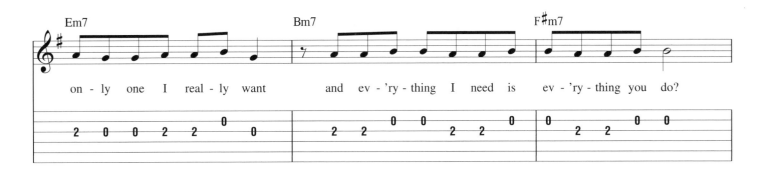

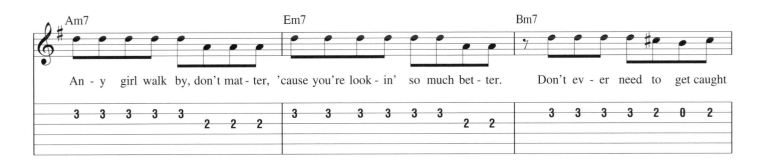

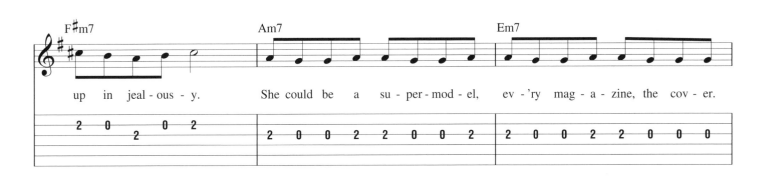

Chorus

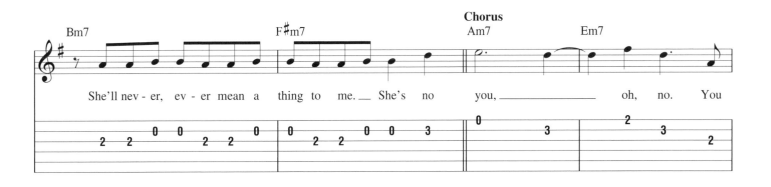

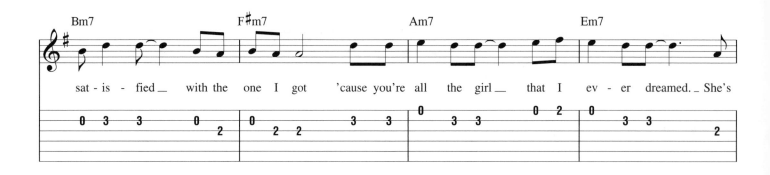

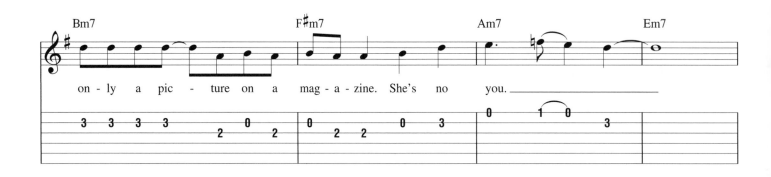

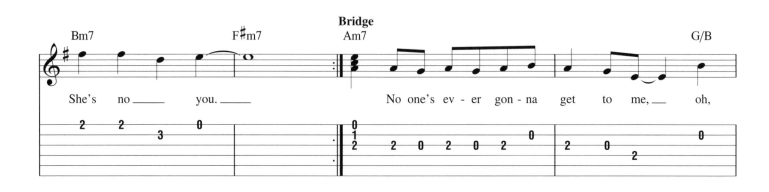

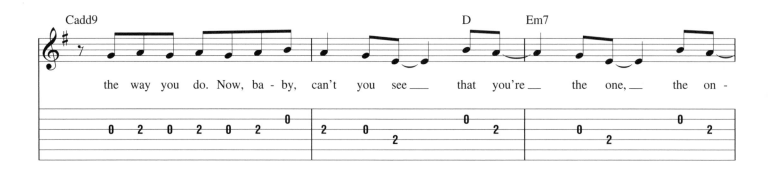

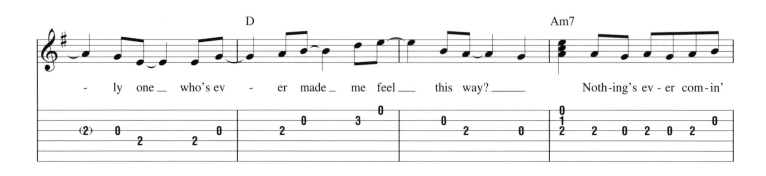

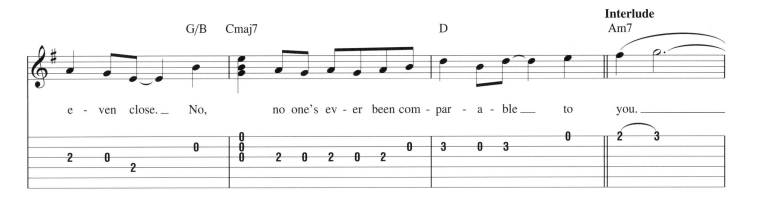

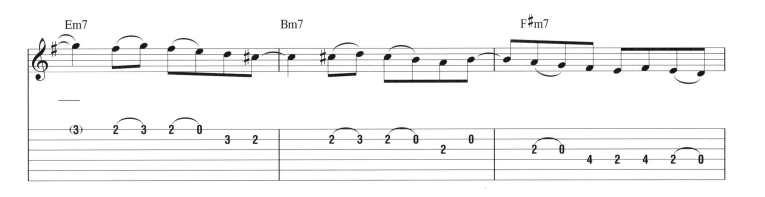

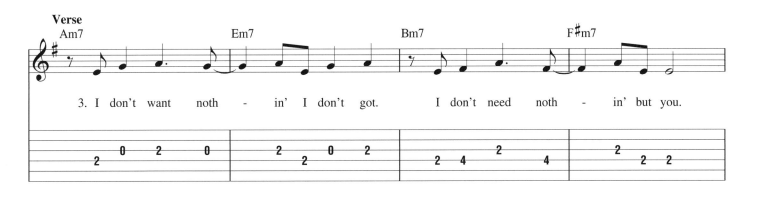

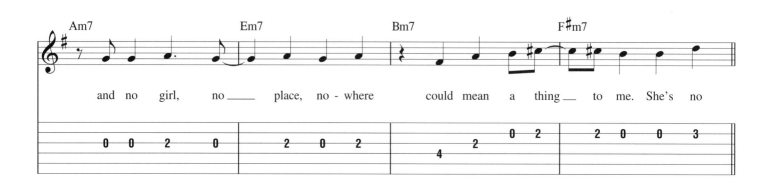

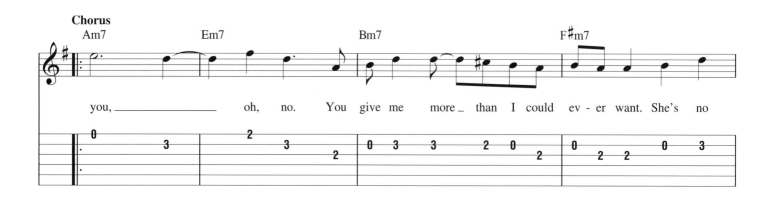

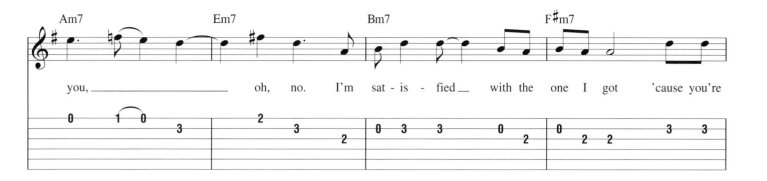

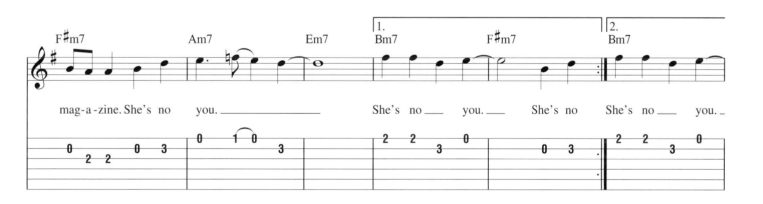

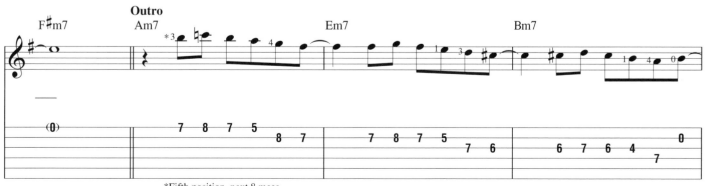

*Fifth position, next 8 meas.

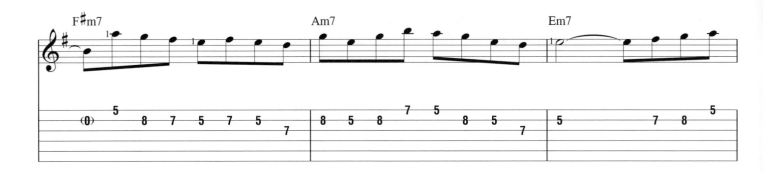

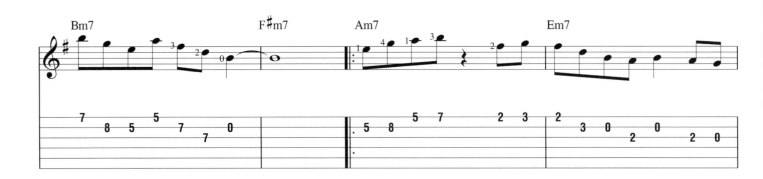

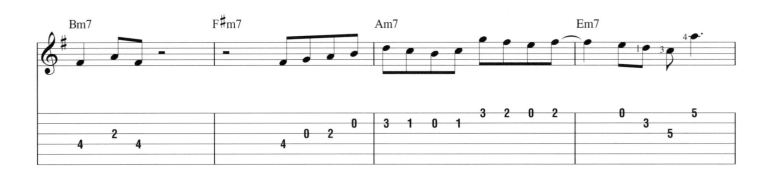

*Fifth position

Additional Lyrics

2. They got a lotta girls who dance in all the videos,
But I prefer the way you do, the way you move.
You're more than beautiful and I just wanna let you know
That all I ever need is what I got with you.
Any girl walk by, don't matter, ev'ry time you're lookin' better.
I think you're perfect; there ain't nothin' I would change.
She could be a super model, ev'ry magazine, the cover.
She'll never, ever take my heart away.

Shining Star

Words and Music by Maurice White, Philip Bailey and Larry Dunn

Strum Pattern: 5, 6
Pick Pattern: 4, 6

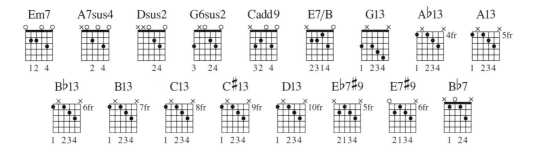

(when you wish up-on a dream), life ain't al-ways what it seems.

Once you see your light so clear, in

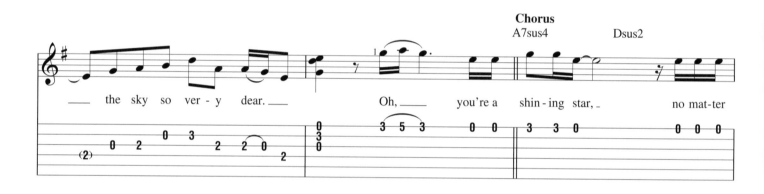

Chorus

A7sus4   Dsus2

the sky so ver-y dear. Oh, you're a shin-ing star, no mat-ter

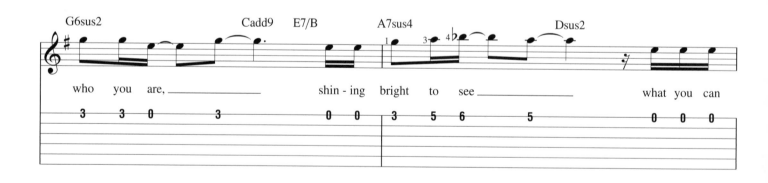

G6sus2   Cadd9 E7/B   A7sus4   Dsus2

who you are, shin-ing bright to see what you can

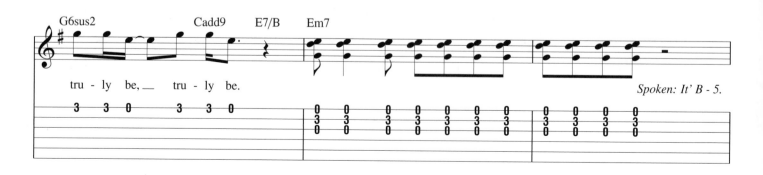

G6sus2   Cadd9 E7/B Em7

tru-ly be, tru-ly be. *Spoken: It' B - 5.*

Verse

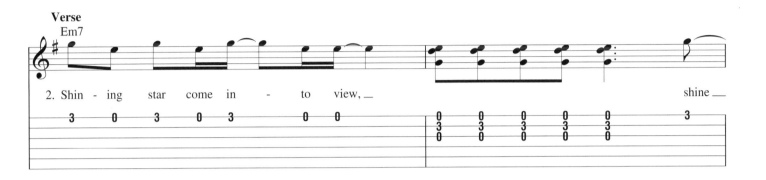

2. Shin - ing star come in - to view, ___ shine ___

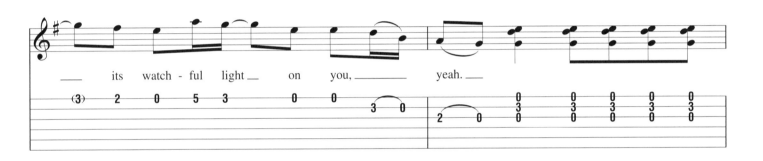

___ its watch - ful light ___ on you, _____ yeah. ___

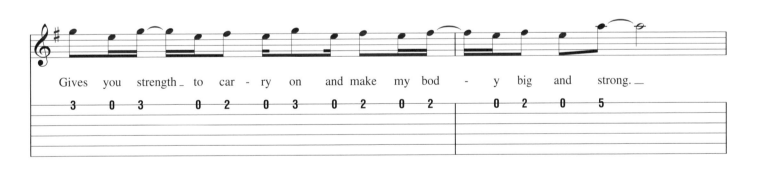

Gives you strength ___ to car - ry on and make my bod ___ y big and strong. ___

On an ad - ven - ture of the sun, ___ it's all a - wake and just ___ be - gun. ___

*Sung one octave higher, next 2 meas.

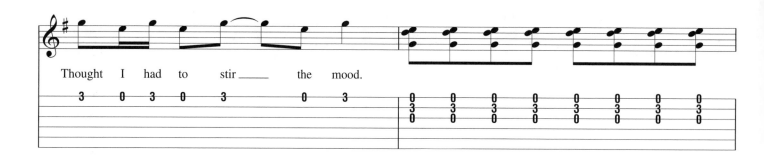

Thought I had to stir _____ the mood.

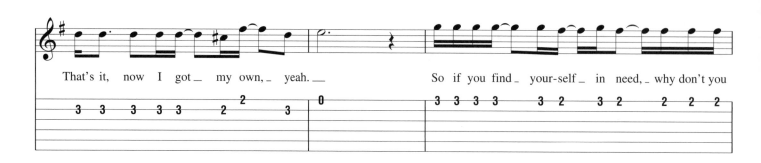

That's it, now I got _ my own, _ yeah. _ So if you find _ your-self _ in need, _ why don't you

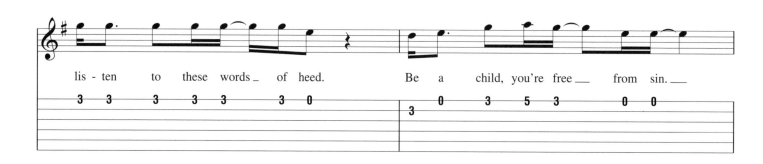

lis - ten to these words _ of heed. Be a child, you're free _____ from sin. _

Outro-Chorus
Em7

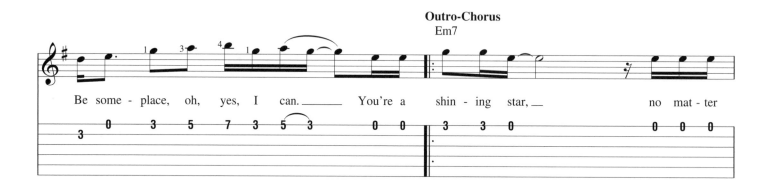

Be some - place, oh, yes, I can. _ You're a shin - ing star, _ no mat - ter

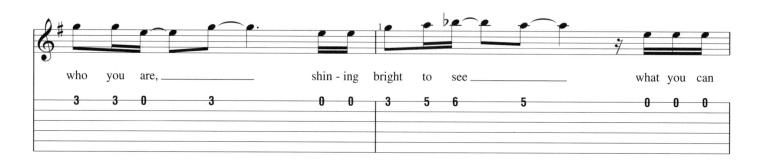

who you are, _____ shin - ing bright to see _____ what you can

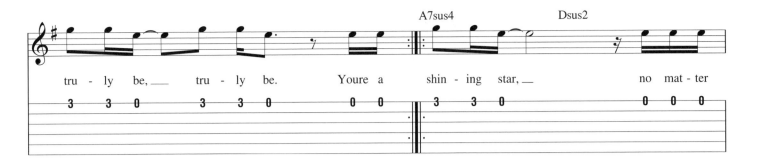

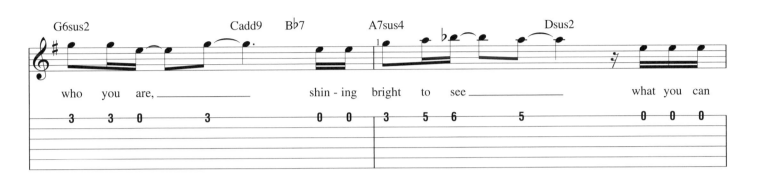

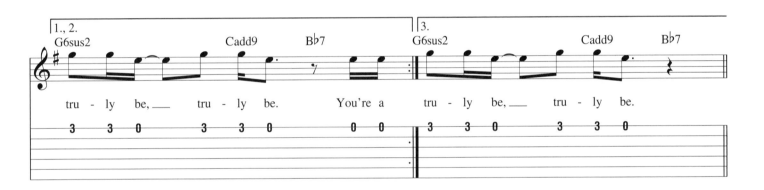

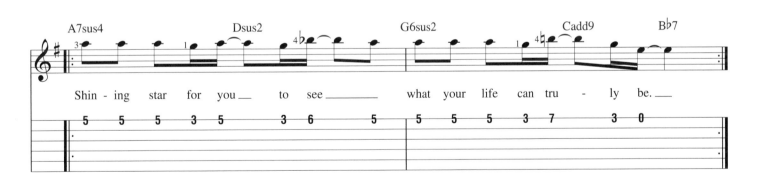

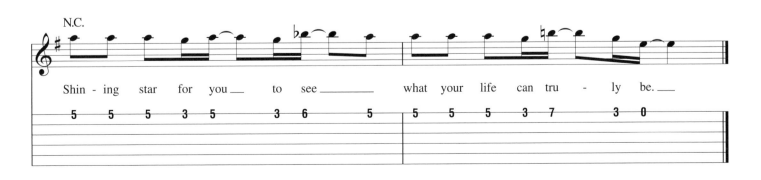

Find Yourself in You

Words and Music by Matthew Gerrard, Amber Hezlep, Julia Ross and Sarah Ross

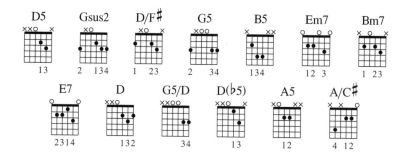

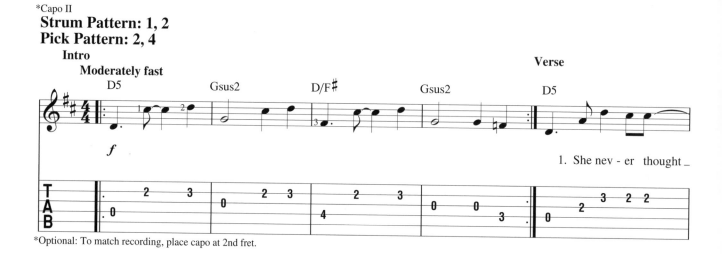

*Capo II

Strum Pattern: 1, 2
Pick Pattern: 2, 4

*Optional: To match recording, place capo at 2nd fret.

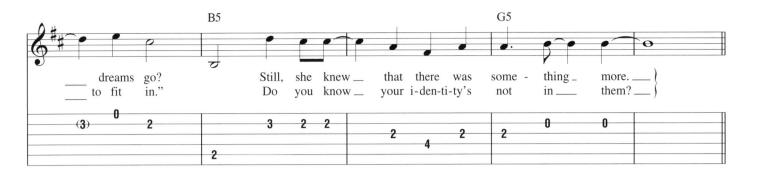

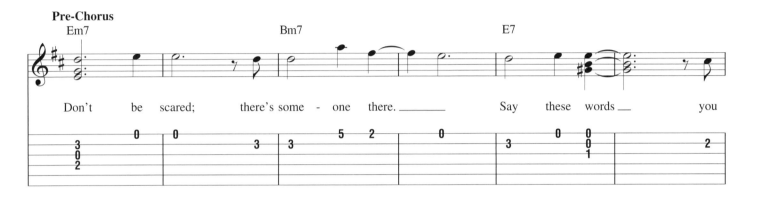

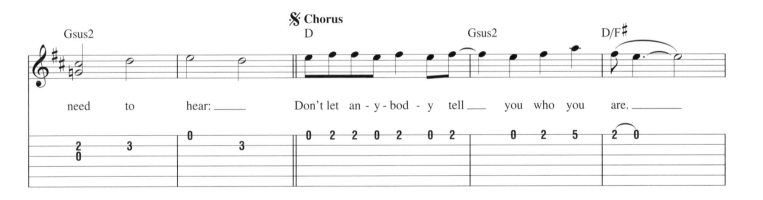

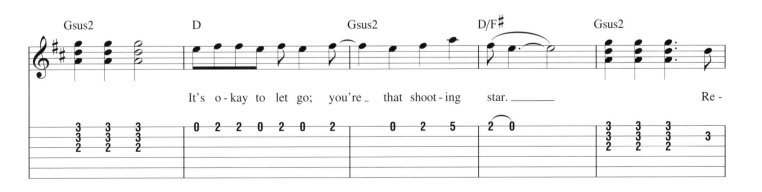

mem - ber all ___ you wished for. Be - lieve it will ___ be true. You will nev - er find your-self ___

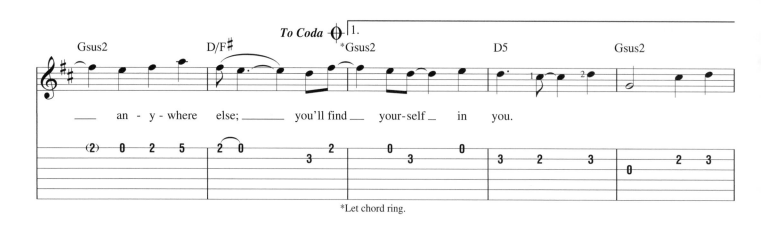

___ an - y - where else; _____ you'll find ___ your-self ___ in you.

*Let chord ring.

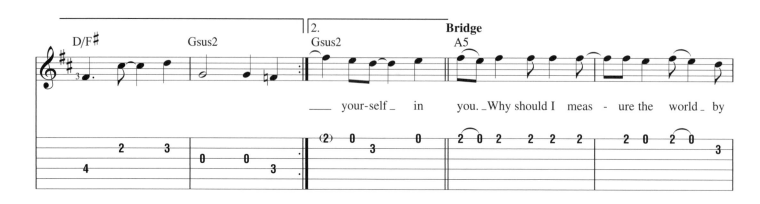

___ your-self _ in you. _Why should I meas - ure the world _ by

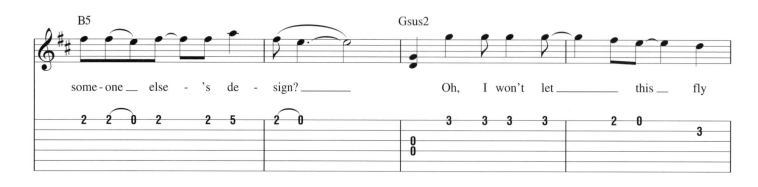

some - one ___ else - 's de - sign? _____ Oh, I won't let _____ this ___ fly

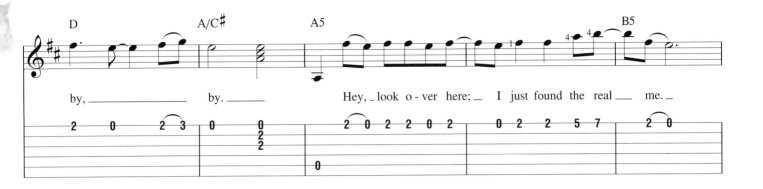

by, _____ by. _____ Hey, _ look o - ver here; _ I just found the real __ me. _

D.S. al Coda

Now it's your turn to see. ____ Now it's your turn to see. ____

⊕ Coda

____ your-self _ in you. You'll find __ your-self _ in you. _

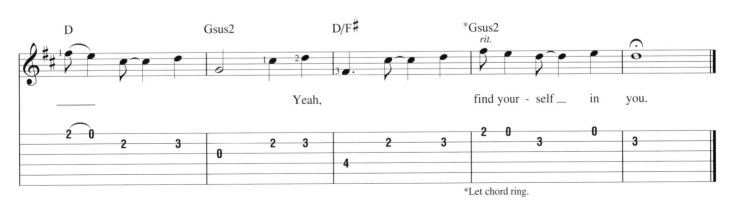

Yeah, find your - self __ in you.

*Let chord ring.

I Learned from You

Words and Music by Matthew Gerrard and Steve Diamond

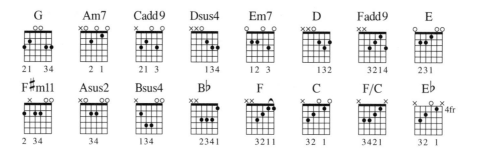

Strum Pattern: 7, 8
Pick Pattern: 7, 8

Intro
Moderately

Verse

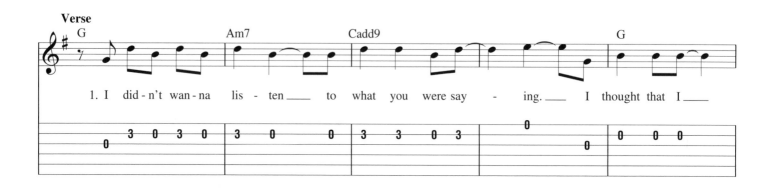

1. I did-n't wan-na lis - ten ___ to what you were say - ing. ___ I thought that I ___

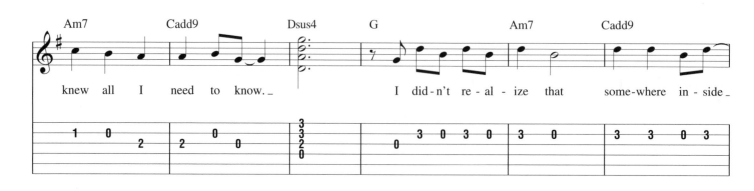

knew all I need to know. _ I did-n't re-al-ize that some-where in-side _

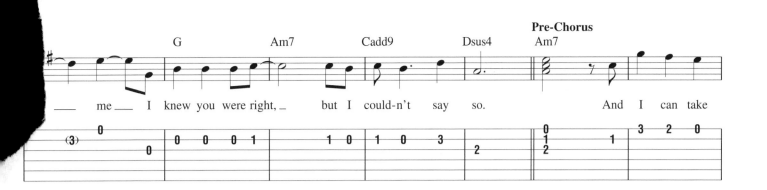

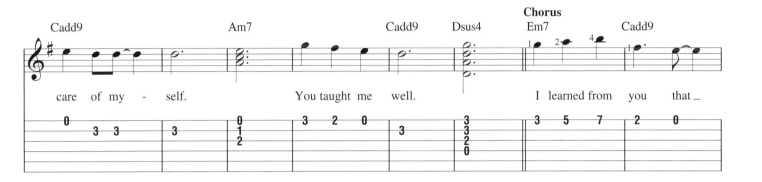

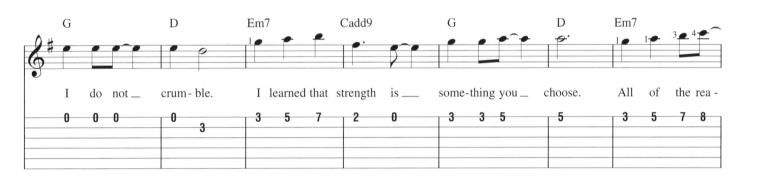

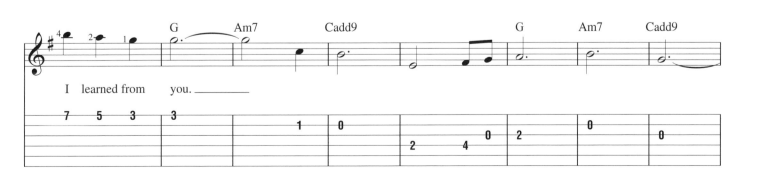

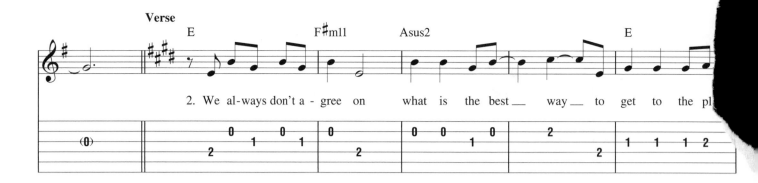

2. We al-ways don't a - gree on   what is   the best ___ way ___ to   get   to   the pl

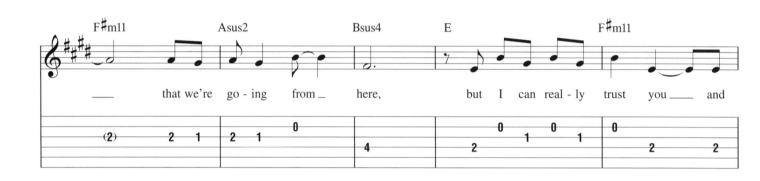

___   that we're go - ing   from ___ here,   but I can real - ly trust you ___ and

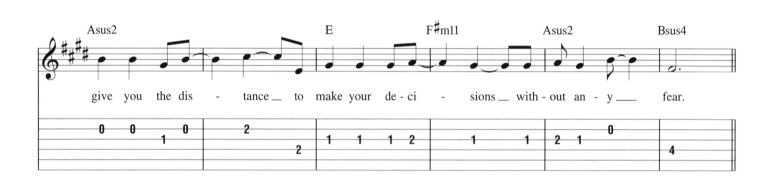

give   you   the dis -   tance ___ to make your de - ci -   sions ___ with - out an - y ___ fear.

Pre-Chorus

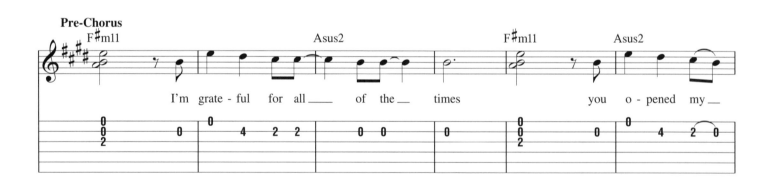

I'm grate - ful   for all ___ of the ___ times   you   o - pened my ___

𝄋 Chorus

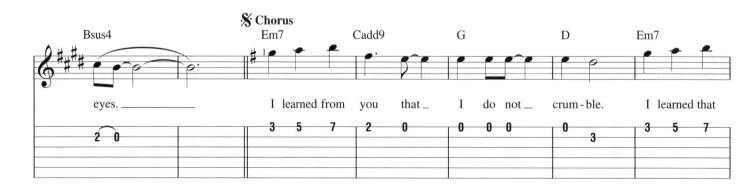

eyes. _____   I learned from   you   that ___ I   do not ___ crum - ble.   I learned that

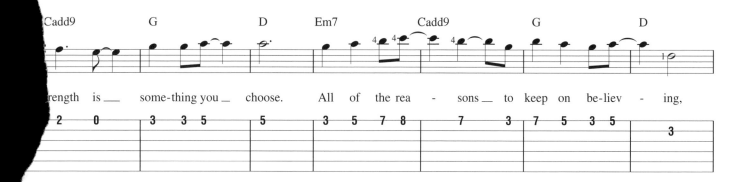

strength is __ some-thing you __ choose. All of the rea - sons __ to keep on be-liev - ing,

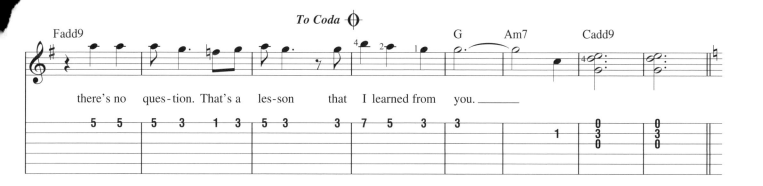

To Coda ⊕

there's no ques-tion. That's a les-son that I learned from you. _____

Bridge

You taught me to stand __ on my __ own, and I thank you for that. __ It

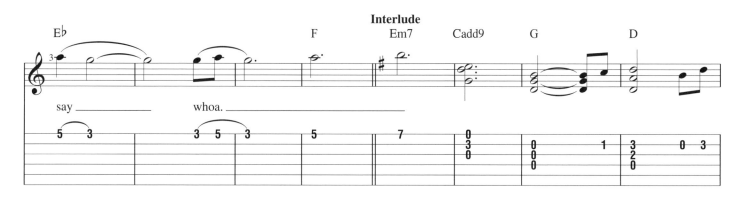

saved me, ___ it made me. And now that I'm __ look - ing back __ I can

Interlude

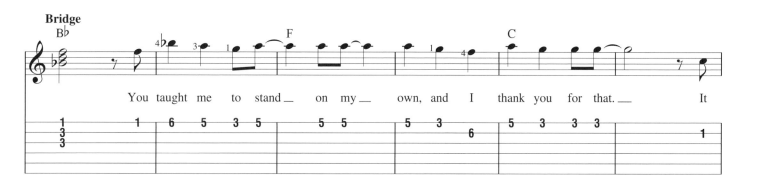

say _____ whoa. _____

Coda

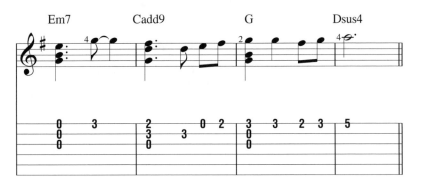

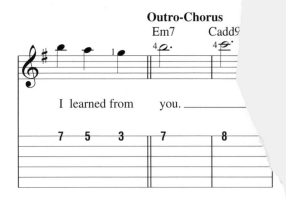

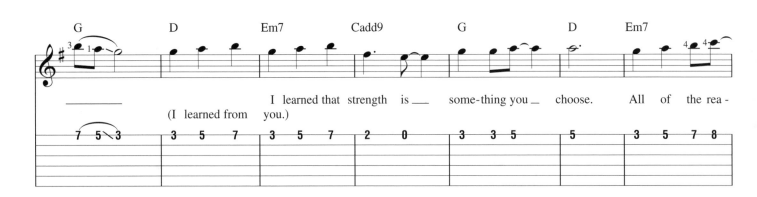

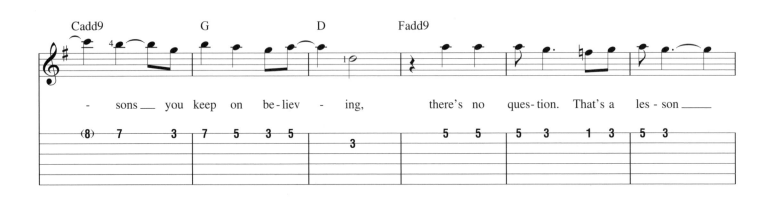

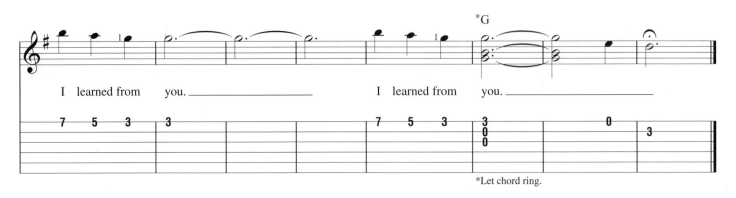

*Let chord ring.